her thoughts

her thoughts

a collection of poetry

Tiffany A. Walker

Copyright © 2025 by Tffany A. Walker

All rights reserved.
No part of this book may be copied, reproduced, or distributed
in any form without written permission from the author, except for brief quotes used in reviews or articles

ISBN 979-8-9850230-0-8

Printed in the United States

To my past, present,
and future
self

poems

Lovely Thoughst

    I... Because... You
    Can I count on you
    Negativity is a mindset
    Humbly kneel
    Together again
    Magnetic love
    What happens next

Painful Thoughts

    Scar
    Storm of sorrow
    Sea of despair
    My defected boomerang
    Bittersweet good-bye
    Love me
    Harsh words are like piercing bullets
    Fleeting magic
    Ticking clock

I'm afraid
Why try and break me
All roads come to an end
Emptiness

Wandering Thoughts

Dreams
Dare you speak
White walls
I write
Final chapter
Seasons
Let's grab a coke
A lesson to be learned
Tradition
Aunt Flo
Fairy tales, farewells
Emotional eating
All that is good to me
Cadabra
Her thoughts

Family Thoughts

Grandpa
This is on me
Forever in my heart, Grandma
Thank you
Wings of comfort
Light as a feather
Maker of me
Fatherless daughter
My loves

introduction

"her thoughts" is a collection of poetry composed over a span of two decades. Poetry was introduced at a pivotal time in my life, at the tender age of thirteen.

As I began to write I was pleasantly surprised to find myself growing a fondness for the art of poetic expression. Not only did I discover my enjoyment of the art form but also my proficiency in the art of verse. From then, words on paper became my avenue for self expression, free of judgment and allowing for self reflection.

Words, as the instruments of my expression, have served as an outlet for countless emotions and deep thoughts. For me, it's the delicate placement of words that invites readers to partake in the spectrum of my innermost sentiment.

The composition of poetry has shown to be an invaluable vehicle, facilitating the articulation of a kaleidoscope of emotions.

Be it the exuberance of joy, the desolation of abandonment, the melancholy of sadness, or the profound ache of heartbreak.

"her thoughts" is a journey through the labyrinth of my psyche revealing the vulnerability of my concealed thoughts. Venturing into the realm of wandering thoughts and capturing thoughts of love, pain, and familial bonds. All of which are inspired by the volatile whims of life's unfolding narrative.

poems

Lovely Thoughts

I...because...you

I need you because I love you,
I love you because I can't be without you,
I can't be without you because I am apart of you,
I am a part of you because I understand you,
I understand you because I hear you,
I hear you because I listen to you,
I listen to you because I am here for you,
I am here for you because I care for you,
I care for you because I believe in you,
I believe in you because I have faith in you,
I have faith in you because I trust you,
I trust you because I know you,
I know you because I adore you,
I adore you because
I love you

can I count on you

If I was hurt would you comfort me
If I was lost would you guide me
If I was weak would you strengthen me
If I was alone would you hold me
If I was sick would you care for me
If I was threatened would you protect me
If I was ignored would you acknowledge me
If I was adventurous would you journey with me
If I was an allusion would you dream of me
If I was unattractive would you still look at me
If I wanted to be heard would you listen to me
If I was a star would you wish upon me
If I was a rainbow would you search for my gold
If I was aching would you soothe me
If my heart was shattered would you glue it back together
If I was dying would you die with me

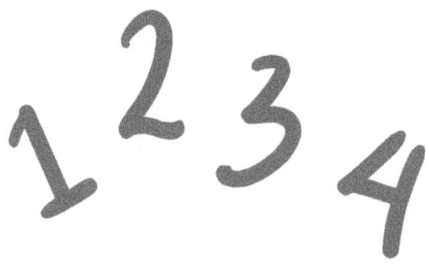

negativity is a mindset

Feed with a silver spoon from a broken platter
When all is lost and dreams have failed nothing really matters
My thoughts are broken and my spirit has been shattered

It is rough living without you but I must look ahead
I turn to God for help as I read my *Daily Bread*
I've read that faith without work is dead
I have faith, I work hard, and still, I get nothing instead

I live today but pay for it tomorrow
I awake happily but go to sleep full of pain, guilt, and sorrow
I will soon find a peace of my own
When my heart becomes my home

Growth is needed and efforts are timeless
I must grasp the understanding that negativity is a mindset

humbly kneel

Graciously kneel, take thy humble knee
There is no sense in fighting, we are the powers that be
I do not wish to leave you, and you wish not to leave me
We live for much more, our bond is of the contrary
We do not wish to live a life filled with the ordinary

Satisfactions of life, live as if this is the best there is to come
Basking in the materials and indulge in all the fun
Oh, for others, life is but a dream, as sweet as the smell of a freshly baked Cinnabon
No need for a sweet treat to pleasure my heart, for those things I do not succumb

My flesh is but a dwelling, my spirit is in command
I see my purpose is much bigger, on a scheme that is grand
I love thy heart, I feel your words, you've helped me understand
I partner with you, let me take thy hand

I need you as my mate, without you, my life would not be complete

With you I desire to connect,
together there is nothing we can't defeat
Our path is overstood,
our ultimate mission is concrete

I am ready for action, our plan is set in stone
I do not fancy solitude, I have no aspirations to be alone
I hold no negative self-infliction
My truth with you is in my ultimate conviction

together again

Deny Destiny
Devour Dignity
Demonstrate Deceitfulness
Babble Blissfully
I love you and you love me
Why is it impossible for us to be
Compare Compassion
In love with lust
But lust for love
I yearn for you holding my soul
And kissing my heart
Apprehensive Attraction
Sensual Satisfaction
Understanding Unity
Torn Truth
Bewildered Betrayal
Lonesome Life
Realistically my chances of having you
Are slim to none
I don't know how this can be overcome
Wanting the situation to be undone
However, do believe that, for you, I am happy
But this loneliness of mine is unsatisfactory

magnetic love

I want you in my life, is that even possible
I am willing to dominate and overcome any obstacle
Together as a team, we are sure to be unstoppable
I am drawn to you magnetically
Your spirit is an array of positive energy
We are meant for each other, we have stable chemistry

what happens next

A speck of gold, a silver kiss
It's not worth more than
the opportunity to reminisce
To have and to hold
With love that overflows
Deceive and distrust
Your eyes filled with lust
Dishonest and disloyal
My anger is beginning to boil
Hate love or love pain
Either way unhappiness remains
Forget or be forgotten
Love is spoiled rotten
Quiver or quench
You simply can't resist
Love all or hate one
The past can never be undone
Cry loud or speak soft
Without you I would have been better off
Substitute or neglect
I see I don't have you respect
Continue on or end now
Who knows what happens next

Painful Thoughts

scar

Pain inflicted that has left you with a scar
And now the pain made you the way that you are
Angry all the time, sour, and bitter
Always giving up on love and becoming a quitter
But you need to learn how to forgive
Because you only have one life to live
You're bound to make a mistake
And there will be risks you're just going to have to take
The scar will no longer be a part of you but a thing of the past
It was there for a long time but never forever will it last

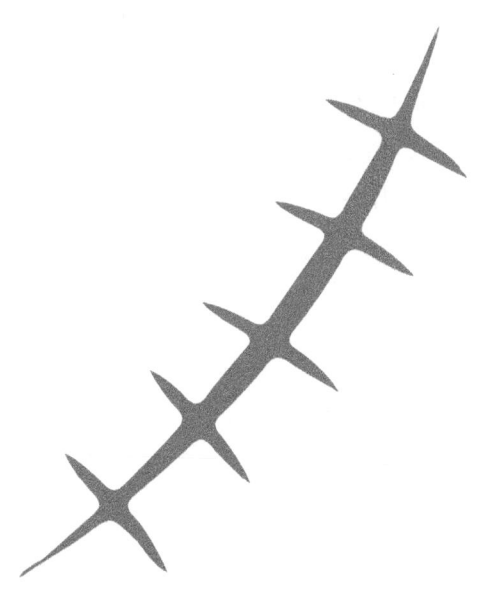

storm of sorrow

A heart of broken sorrow
Love deep and strong each day
like there is no tomorrow

Death can not do us part
Because the mate to my soul
will take shelter in my heart

Why not just embrace what is mine
no matter how many cloudy days come,
my sun will still shine

I find myself suffering from
the misfortunes of you once more
Lavish upon our souls a chance to implore

The ending is hopeless so why
even entertain the thought
It will be like trying to dodge raindrops

sea of despair

Looking for hope but it is nowhere to be found
Should I come up for air or let myself drown
Sinking beneath the surface with my tears all around
Having these undesirable thoughts always gets me down
If only there was a way to smile, so I wouldn't wear a frown

I wonder why this is the way it has come to be
Searching for answers that are lost at sea
Bonded to depression, but wanting be free
Locked in a house of pain, seeking the missing key
Never having the ability to safely flea
Knowing what's next to come, the future I can foresee
Just as I suspected, depression always finds me

my defected boomerang

I don't want to let go, however, my hand is losing grip
I'm not so sure you will come back but away you begin to slip
I raise my arm, first pulling back then launching forward releasing you into the air
Hoping the directions are correct, not quite certain which leaves my heart in despair

Is it true that no matter what, to your owner you will always return?
What if you get lost, how would you find me, these are the questions of my biggest concern
How is this going to work, you weren't exactly new, you were someone else's before
I just couldn't say no because there is something about you I adore

Away you go and here I stay
Hoping soon you will return to me for one more play
As I stand there waiting for you, hoping, it suddenly hit me in a blink of an eye
I saw you coming in my direction, with my hands open, you simply flew right by
I tilted my head, collected my emotions and departed

Now I know undoubtedly they always end up where they first started

bittersweet good-bye

Deluded depression
Fidget frustrations
Awkward arrival
Defaulted departure
This is without a doubt not how it's supposed to be
What the future holds for you and I is not up to me
To accept that what I loved and adored most was taken from me
I thank you even though you left me heartbroken and torn
You gave me roses, then ripped them from my hands, now I bleed because of thorns
It's funny because we had a beautifully awkward hello and a bittersweet good-bye

love me

Kiss me where I've never been kissed
Grab me where you won't lose grip
Hold me 'til your arms become numb
Soothe me 'til my skin grow soft

Talk to me 'til you run out of breath
Look at me 'til your eyes grow tired
Listen to me as I talk you to death
Lift my spirit before you let me down

Come closer before you walk away
Acknowledge me before you ignore me
Respect me before you neglect me
Break up with me if you wish to wonder

Be honest, never lie to me
Treat me with dignity, never do me dirty
Tell me everything, never keep secrets
If anything... love me, never hate me

I've told you all that I want you to do
Please make me happy and all my
dreams come true

harsh words are like piercing bullets

As I open my heart to you, consciously you stab me with your words
My utterance is spoken with tranquility but the articulation of your rage is absurd
You viciously attack me with the anger in your thought
I catch your every word like a bullet a soul caught
I speak at a distance, miles away the fury in your gut retrieves me, still I am shot down
I see your wrath but my reluctant audacity dare me to speak, my voice is without sound

It's not what you say but how you say it, that changes the significance of the expression
My emotions are scarce but my thoughts flow like a river, afraid for my essence
I pose at a halt, my words are in a recession
Even my halt can not protect my sentiment from the intensity of your penetration
Ambushed when I'm already down as if you like to see me continuously bleed sadness and aggravation

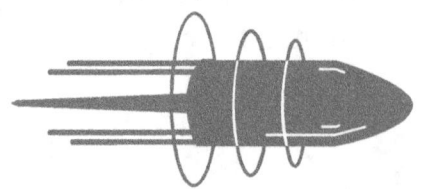

fleeting magic

I feel our magic is disappearing as we forget to believe and acknowledge that it is real
Magic is a gesture of our imagination, as long as we believe, it is something we can feel
Our days are not the same anymore
Our words lack the compassion and admiration as they did before
You no longer caress my heart with the utterance of endearment
I crave true love but the thought of it is merely an imperfection of the mind
It's truly magically and rather hard to come by

ticking clock

I say I wouldn't cry but I do it every day
I thought you'd make me happy and my loneliness would go away
I tried my hardest to make it right but it ends up being all wrong
Why do I try to make it work, knowing we were never meant all along
Even knowing I still vie for you, ignoring the fact that it feels awkward
Still I persist, turning like clockwork

I fear our time is growing shorter, and soon, you and I will be over
If only I could have found a way to make us closer the hourglass empties and I'm at it again
I dread what comes next, we were better off as friends
But I just couldn't help liking you and wanting you as my man

Thinking you were different but, realized you're like them all
I liked you instantly which made it easy for me to fall

I lost track of time and much of it was wasted
Chasing a love that wasn't fated

I give and give only to get nothing in return
Second time, second chance, second love, second hurt but still I have yet to learn
Maybe I would be better if I stay in my thoughts kept tucked away in a box
I must make a choice soon, the time on the clock won't stop
Deep down in my heart I know we are not cut out, sad but true
Maybe it's time to part ways, and say goodbye to you

I'm afraid

I'm afraid you will do the same thing you did before
I'm afraid you and I will be no more

I'm afraid you will end our relationship
I'm afraid I will no longer be able to kiss your lips

I'm afraid our happy days will soon be gone
I'm afraid I will soon be alone

I'm afraid you will find happiness with someone else
I'm afraid this will happen and I am left by myself

I'm afraid I won't open myself up to you more
I'm afraid on our relationship you will close the door

I'm afraid you will fall for another girl
I'm afraid I will no longer be a part of your world

I'm afraid your love for me will soon fade
I need you to help me because I am afraid

why try and break me

I don't know what you're implying, but I know who I am
If you don't accept me, then you're not meant to be my man
I am not conceded and I am not trying to be miss independent
If have to, I can be, but that's not what I intended
All you like to do is talk down and condescend
I see for you, playing games seems to be a recurring trend

I am confident in myself as well as my abilities
We could build a home of a lifetime, filled with all the top amenities
I know my worth which is why I won't stand for hostilities
I know how to commit and handle my responsibilities
I am not for the bickering and arguing, I hate toxicity
So sticking around for the negativity...
it's a low probability

I treat you like a king when you enter our castle
I ease your mind and make you forget about all your day's hassle

Out there, it's you against the world, in here, we work as one
We work as halves but together we can get it all done
We are made to be attached
We can work but we have to have each other's back

Ideally, I envision a future as such
Hunted by our past we can't amount to much
Denial to the truth as if we can change our cards
To walk away now would be devastating and hard

I have experienced the fades of your touch and the drift of your voice
Unfortunately in a bind, and left without a choice
Slain by the blow of your downplay, collaborating with my newly found self-doubt
I have awakened to the understanding that I may be better off without

all roads come to an end

My intentions are never to cause problems
I don't know about you but I don't like to be lied to
At this point I'm not sure what it is I am to do
I have this information but how do I put it to use
I confront you, but you lie until your face turns blue
And still, deny every bit like this is something that isn't true

Innocent until proven guilty but your guilt doesn't phase
You speak direct lies right into my face
Always good to try to reverse the case
Mouthpiece special, dressed up fancy and finished with lace
I fell for the washed and reused lines like I was blinded by mace
One after the other, you continue to hold your pace

I come to you with the utmost respect
But my vulnerability has been offered and left with neglect
If you don't see where I come from then I don't see where we connect

Emptiness

I have a void
I try to avoid
That remains unhealed
With emptiness living I've learned to deal
I see joy all around that I want to steal
But it's not mine to feel
So it wouldn't be real
If only I could have taken it and truly enjoyed
Unfortunately this mental state has internally destroyed

Wandering Thoughts

dreams

Dreams are nothing more than what you image
You can dream of anything like love and sweet passion
I dream I would get married to a loving man
Who will want me to be his wife until the very end
And would care about me and how I feel
Let me know that his love for me is genuinely real
He will understand me as a woman and adore me as his wife
He will do anything for me and satisfy my needs in life
Being a great husband isn't as hard as it may seem
Maybe it will happen for me one day, but for now, it is just a dream

dare you speak

Why are men placed before women
But ladies before gentlemen
Women are forced by society
To cross their legs and sit quietly
While men are being glorified
By the lights of ideology
It bothers me
That your mind had the capacity
To cultivate a perception full of audacity
You masterfully created a culture in your favor
Do savor
the flavor
of your sweet victory
The misfortune of it is everlasting
because I am not taught her story but his story
my identity is not handcrafted by myself but by the manufacturer's embroidery
It's destroying me that I must live amongst those who, from a woman's canal, rose
And will manifest gestures of maleficence
Birthed the inclination that we all wanted to exist under a dictatorship

Don't be my enemy, instead be my teammate
Together we embody the ultimate relationship
Our ship won't sail but part ways until you finally come to the realization
My cry is the source of your condensation
My exhale gives headway to the nourishment of your essence
My mood predetermines the lay of the land, but not even the nature of my consequence have taught you any lessons

white walls

My thoughts are amused by the emptiness of this room
Layered with hopelessness covered in gloom
As I sit here alone I am compelled to think
Longing for love, my heart begins to sink
Submerged in compromising thoughts
Yearning for luxuries that can't be bought
Clenching onto a host of imperfect emotions
Free flowing thoughts, let's paint an ocean
Crashing waves like my fears that roar
Wiped out like false listener and slamming doors
Drowning in pain I beg that my heart be spared
So that I may visualize a beachside sunset to share
I try to veil the truth of my heart as I am unselfishly running
Irresistibly drawn to an emptiness far too cunning

I write

Free of negativity, free of pain
My destiny remains,
Intact
As a matter of fact
My legacy will not be the death of me
Why must death bring forth my legacy
I search long and hard but nothing is what I find
I must master a skill
Or I will
Be washed away in time
Left with not even a speck of dust but a crumby sign
Marking my position beneath the feet
Of those who seek
To master
A disaster
They call life
Forgive me for my strife
Don't get it twisted because I am one to fight
against all odds
Even the rumbles of thunder and lightning rods
It gives me the power to push and regain my stands
Because I demand
The rights to my dreamland
I shall live in greatness as I walk this Earth
The universe marked me special at the
time of my birth

final chapter

Going on thirty years, I have been subdued to what is considered a human form
Reluctant to exist in the conditions, I have been outnumbered and forced to conform

My conformity does not defy my morality
because in all actuality
we are an illusion
Mislead by implication of free will, my mind tainted, now altered by the intrusion

"They" will remain nameless, hopefully, you follow me, catch my drift downstream
Hold tight because although as ambiguous as my statement may seem
Life is to be lived with the mindset of one theme

50 cent said it best, "Get rich or die trying."
dying
is not an option… at least not yet
Purposely placed, my journey is not fulfilled,
but it will,
because to this life I am a vet

This is my last and final walk on Earth, I do not wish to return
I am destined for greatness,
I will settle for nothing less
Settlement is beneath me,
I will rise above as I ascend
I will transcend
because I am neither man nor woman...
I have God within

seasons

I imagine to sit beneath the trees
Watching as grass comfort falling leaves
Silently listening to the chirp of birds
and the buzzing bees
Salvaging ants, the whistling breeze,
Humid air, and penetrating sunbeams
I am tickled by butterflies as they flutter their wings
The beauties of life my favorites of Fall and Spring
I find enjoyment awaiting for all that life has to bring

let's grab a Coke

Your friendship has been delicious and refreshing
You are the best friend my heart ever had
Your heart is pure as sunlight
It's the real thing
You can't beat the feeling
It had to be good to get where it is

I want to sit on the beach with you,
have a coke and a smile
All the pauses that refreshes
Taste the feeling
The cold, crisp taste
We look at each other with a sign of good taste
Life tastes good

a lesson to be learned

Getting really tired cause I've been walking in the heat
I'm going to a friends house not to far from my street
A man slowed down to ask if I needed a ride
I should have said no, just one little white lie
Slowly I opened the door and got into the car
I figured this would be quick since I wasn't going far
Just a few blocks away, I'll be there in no time
I noticed he locked the doors but I paid it no mind

We passed my friend's street, he didn't let me out
I panicked, didn't know what to do so I began to shout
I know he seen the scared look that grew upon my face
So he started to go faster as if he was in a Nascar race

This began to not be such a good decision anymore
We came to a stop and I was lead to a door
It opened then we began to walk down creaky narrow stairs
My mind wandered and I conjured up many scares
Like if I went missing would anyone notice, would they even care
And ideas of what he might do

Maybe something mean and grotesque then finish the job by ending me too
He tied both of my arms and legs to the railings of a bed
The only part of my body I was able to move freely was head
As he stood and stared I could see the coldness in his eyes
Hopelessly, I laid my head back and cried

Unable to run, I was lost and afraid
With nothing left to do I closed my eyes and prayed
For a miracle to convince this man let me go
If I ever get set free I know riding in cars with strangers is a definite No-No

tradition

To you and yours, as the clock strikes the hour
And hungry faces begin to devour
The home-cooked heartfelt meals
As the night rolls on full of laughter and great thrills
Humbled to be reserved
Quite thankful to have traditions preserved

Imagining life without would be such a shame
As we move forward we begin to forget the names
Of those who have come before
Giving up their lives as they opened doors
we are afraid to walkthrough
as we hold dear to the refusal to learn what is true

We use slavery as a crutch
because we feel we can't amount to much
More than what the master has shown,
while we dim the fire of what's innately known
We once walked the Earth as Kings and Queens
We are the ultimate Beings

But we sit around and indulge in holidays that have no place in our original tradition
We took a plea deal as we collectively decided to condition

Conform to the man
Not living life for ourselves or formulating a contentious plan
Our minds and fullest potential will remain dormant
Because we have decided to forfeit
Our spirits to toxic lies
Feed to us by a people with "blonde hair and blue eyes"
Who believe they are the superior race
We bow our heads to them as they spit in our face
But who am I to judge
I just can't sit still because my spirit gave me a nudge

aunt flo

She always visits when I least expect it,
I must put her on my schedule or her arrival,
I will forget it
Her stay is short and to the point, Still I need much preparation, two weeks to be exact
I must set an alarm for when she is to come, just to keep track

My stomach undoubtedly will feel inflated like a balloon
I will give a hard past on any social events, instead, I will stay home and cocoon
My mood will change from being happy to possessing sadness and gloom
Her energy gives me an overwhelmingly rush of hormones,
Please forgive me, my actions mean know malice
And chocolate seems to be the only thing that will satisfy my palette

Her entire wardrobe consists of articles of red
And when it spills over, everything it touches I want to shred
You have a 28-day cycle from start to finish
Oh how I am so eager to see 50 so her visits will diminish

Her first visit caught me by surprise
Dapper in my school uniform until her facetious acts came to vandalize

She took an innocence that I, unfortunately, cannot retract
I must hide her when she arrives, if she is ever spotted I will be given so much flak
She comes with an abundance of pain that I must carry on my back

The burden of her existence, the beauty of her pain
The creation in her name is why she is so famed
I now understand her purpose even though hormones are extraordinarily progressive
And I can never get comfortable with her presence, it's a bit annoying and excessive

I do love it when I have a 9-to-10-month break
Anything extra after that is just icing on the cake
That I whipped up for my bun in the oven
Made with special care and a whole lot of lovin'
She comes and goes, that's fine and swell
Until next time, so long, and farewell

fairy tales, farewells

The complications of complicated and the defeat of it all
Love builds bridges and heartache builds walls
Looking for my knight in shining armor, instead I find a night of glimmering darkness
Like all things, enjoy it while it last because soon it too will fade
Time and time again we are fascinated by the idea to be
With someone loving us more than we

Depicted by once upon of times and happily ever after's
Love is more than what we think, it changes even faster
Than we can blink our eyes or what we feel deep within
The best person to fall in love with, they say, is with a friend

If just for one moment, to relive the first time we met
After that thought, you go back to regret

Not everyone shares my interpretation
Love is an experience of all sensations
But the single life has began to receive glorification

I am stuck in old times
The world is evolving and I am behind enemy lines
I know love is not as easy as once upon of time
I still dream to live a life from a fairy tale
I will not let love die and simple say so long farewell

emotional eating

Danish in hand, I love something sweet
After a hard day's work I deserve a rewarding treat
It's nice and satisfying as I rage like a bull
I find myself engorged as I stuff my mouth full

Judge me not for I deserve every crumb
I require a pick-me-up as I lay sunken in a slum
I find it quite satisfying, so tasteful and warm
Just a few more bites shall do me no harm

Covered in chocolate, drizzled on top
I find myself going back for more, it's quite hard to stop
I must keep eating until I bloat and my pants button pop
I don't want to feel my pains, so I keep eating until I drop

Laying still in a diabetic coma
The only thing to get me going is the smell of the sweet baked aroma
Once I awake I'm back at it again
I find comfort in my food, because it's my one truest friend

all that is good to me

I love to sway my hips to the sound of rhythmic tunes; it makes me feel free
I love to belt out my favorite song, it makes me feel exhilarated
I admire the creativity one can display through art, it is a treat to my eyes
I love the taste of exotic foods, it tickles my taste buds

I love the crackling sounds of falling leaves, it makes me feel warm inside
I like to inhale the breath of nature; it makes me feel calm
I am an adrenaline junky, and hiking gets it done, I feel on top of the world
I'd like to have a cup of tea, it makes me feel soothed and relaxed

I want to travel the world, it makes me feel like an explorer
I like to experiment with flavors while cooking, it makes me feel like a scientist
I am excited by vivid reading, it makes me feel imaginative
I like to draw whatever comes to mind, it makes me feel like a creator

I enjoy writing to express myself, it makes me feel relieved
I like to share a good laugh, it makes me feel lifted
I like to think I'm especially skilled, it makes me feel gifted
I love to see when others smile, it makes me feel enjoyed

cadabra

There are perks to being a member
That are far better than any contender
Unlimited music, movies, and books
Exclusive deals that will have you hooked
Most importantly front door delivery of your goods
No discrimination, they even go to the hoods

I'm intrigued by the delivery
Mostly provided with a two day probability
Although arriving early is always a possibility
Privileged with the convenience, I submit orders consistently
Addicted to the nonsense of this trickery

Type in the item name and scroll all day
Add to the cart and then you pay
Just a tap of a button
No time to wait because all of a sudden
I receive a notification on my phone
I check at my door and my package is at my home

her thoughts

Silence is in high demand
Painful thoughts I want to ban
Wandering thoughts I cannot stand
Often experienced, I see them firsthand
Thoughts of family hoping to understand
Subjected to shortcomings I need a helping hand
Lovely thoughts are encouraged to be the lay of the land
Endless means for them to expand
Powerfully perceived and
Always in command

Family Thoughts

grandpa

It has been such an honor
I've seen it as a privilege
To help you on the way out
When you helped me on the way in
You are the greatest man I've ever known
You always smiled even when life went wrong
You lived with so much love
And your presences was such a cheer
I will continue to always smile
Because I know your love is always near

this is on me

My spirit was broken
I'm not ready to bare a child
My love is depleted
I wasn't ready to give you my heart
My battery of life is in no condition
To give you a jump start at life

forever in my heart, grandma

You will be loved and forever missed by family and friends
It was too soon for your life to end
But now you will be with God walking hand in hand
You didn't die you were laid to rest
Although I am sad this happened for the best
Now your in heaven with your mother
There, you will no longer have to suffer
We will remember the special times we had with you
And all the rough times you helped us get through
It's hard to say goodbye
When we think of you we all want to cry
But now, you are pain free
And in heaven, you will forever be

thank you

You helped me with my problems and to overcome my fears
When I cried you were always there to wipe away my tears
You encouraged me with fun and joyful cheers
You made me laugh until I burst into happy tears

You told me to always say what I feel
Never to lie about anything and to always be authentically real
Nobody was able to help me the way you did
You would always treat me special like I was your favorite grandkid

You told me to go after my dreams
Told me I could be anything I wanted to be despite how hard it may seem
You reminded me how great I would be
All I had to do was wait and see

This is why I thank you to this very day

wings of comfort

Instead of gliding within the sky lurking upon innocent prey
You pray upon my innocence and protect me throughout my day
Without you here in the flesh, I feel vulnerable and my heart is not at ease
I need you to wrap your wings around me and hold me close, could you please
My sentiment is broken, lost, and torn
I've held onto you since the day I was born
Every since you left, I have been all alone
No one to call when I want to talk on the phone
I needed you as a kid and even still when I'm grown
I still speak to you and I see you respond
I miss you dearly and love you to infinity and beyond

light as a feather

Today is a day I will mourn forever
I will always cherish the time we spent together
To have had you in my life is a gift I will always treasure
The amount of care you have shown was endless, it is not something anyone can measure

You were a man who wore many hats, you were smart and you were clever
You overcame obstacles by way of transformation from past time error
And became a man who walked by faith in which never wavered whatsoever
You seen many storms but with God you were protected from the weather
You possessed much strength and would never fold under pressure

For us to emulate your character will be a challenge, something we will endeavor
Your mind was filled with wisdom, understanding, and skill, you were smart as ever
Never stingy with your craft you wanted to share it with whoever
Spilling out knowledge to us all, I saw you as a professor

To no longer have you in the presence is much of a displeasure
Away from here you left to go somewhere better
At the weighing of your heart, I undoubtedly know it was as light as a feather

maker of me

You say you love me and you care
But when I need you, you're not there
Having opportunities to spend time together grew rare
Years of my brokenness is quite hard to repair
Your time has be devoted to one person not willing to share

You always speak about us being best friends
But when have you ever tried to amend
Full of excuses and no time to spend
Hardly ever around for me and I couldn't understand
But now I see your brokenness and your desperate need for a man
I have learned many things and now I am my own woman
And I am happy to be where I stand

No ill will towards you or the ways of our relationship
You still have yet to change but I no longer trip
I am at a point in time where I can choose to stay, or dip
A wise person gave me advice and I held on to their tip

You've shown me who you are and I see you loud and clear
I've awakened from my fairytale dreaming now it's time to switch gears

The desire for us to have a great relationship is now in the rear
I will be a fool to expect a change after all these years
My eyes will wither away if I continued to give you anymore of my tears

I will never take away the fact that if it wasn't for you there would be nowhere for me to begin
I thank you for all that you have taught me, now I can go on and win
There will come a time in your life when that regret sinks in
Luckily for you, I can never turn my back on you because we are forever the closest of kin
No matter how much you've hurt me, I will always love you to the end

fatherless daughter

I wish you could have stayed a while
The sight of you would have made me smile
You were only given twenty years
Now I live the rest for your in tears
I am often told I am your reflection
If only I was gifted your affection
I want to question God but I give no objection
I wish you were here so I could feel your protection

I'd like to thank you for my creation
Understand my pain but see my appreciation
Not having you in my life has been a devastation
Staying here with me should have been your obligation
My heart hurts because you're not around
The emptiness of memories with you gets me down
Please watch over me as a proud father
But for me, it sucks living as a fatherless daughter

my loves

You are the highlight of my day
You give me purpose and a will to stay
A true definition of love unconditional
Although you didn't come in a way that is traditional
Fact is, you're here, and all else is dismissible

You have taught me a great deal of patience
Understanding beyond your years you have been so gracious
From the days that we first met
I have loved hard with no regrets
If it ends up being a life with just us
You guys' love is just enough
I won't complain or put up a fuss